Real-World STEM:
Develop Fusion Energy

Real-World STEM: Develop Fusion Energy

Kathryn Hulick

San Diego, CA

For more information, contact:
ReferencePoint Press, Inc.
PO Box 27779
San Diego, CA 92198
www.ReferencePointPress.com

LIBRARY OF CONGRESS CATALOGING-IN-PUBLICATION DATA

Name: Hulick, Kathryn.
Title: Real-World STEM: Develop Fusion Energy/by Kathryn Hulick.
Description: San Diego, CA: ReferencePoint Press, Inc., 2018. | Series:
    Real-World STEM | Audience: Grade 9 to 12. | Includes bibliographical
    references and index.
Identifiers: LCCN 2017011705 (print) | LCCN 2017015109 (ebook) | ISBN
    9781682822463 (eBook) | ISBN 9781682822456 (hardback)
Subjects: LCSH: Fusion reactors—Juvenile literature. | Nuclear
    energy—Juvenile literature. | Nuclear power plants—Juvenile literature.
Classification: LCC TK9204 (ebook) | LCC TK9204 .H85 2018 (print) | DDC
    621.48/4--dc23
LC record available at https://lccn.loc.gov/2017011705

CONTENTS

Great Engineering Achievements

1. Electrification
Vast networks of electricity provide power for the developed world.

2. Automobile
Revolutionary manufacturing practices made cars more reliable and affordable, and the automobile became the world's major mode of transportation.

3. Airplane
Flying made the world accessible, spurring globalization on a grand scale.

4. Water Supply and Distribution
Engineered systems prevent the spread of disease, increasing life expectancy.

5. Electronics
First with vacuum tubes and later with transistors, electronic circuits underlie nearly all modern technologies.

6. Radio and Television
These two devices dramatically changed the way the world receives information and entertainment.

7. Agricultural Mechanization
Numerous agricultural innovations led to a vastly larger, safer, and less costly food supply.

8. Computers
Computers are now at the heart of countless operations and systems that impact people's lives.

9. Telephone
The telephone changed the way the world communicates personally and in business.

10. Air Conditioning and Refrigeration
Beyond providing convenience, these innovations extend the shelf life of food and medicines, protect electronics, and play an important role in health care delivery.

Highways

Forty-four thousand miles of US highways enable personal travel and the wide distribution of goods.

Spacecraft

Going to outer space vastly expanded humanity's horizons and resulted in the development of more than sixty thousand new products on Earth.

Internet

The Internet provides a global information and communications system of unparalleled access.

Household Appliances

These devices have eliminated many strenuous and laborious tasks.

Imaging

Numerous imaging tools and technologies have revolutionized medical diagnostics.

Health Technologies

From artificial implants to the mass production of antibiotics, these technologies have led to vast health improvements.

Laser and Fiber Optics

Their applications are wide and varied, including almost simultaneous worldwide communications, noninvasive surgery, and point-of-sale scanners.

Petroleum and Petrochemical Technologies

These technologies provided the fuel that energized the twentieth century.

Nuclear Technologies

From splitting the atom came a new source of electric power.

High-Performance Materials

They are lighter, stronger, and more adaptable than ever before.

Source: Wm. A. Wulf, "Great Achievements and Grand Challenges," National Academy of Engineering, *The Bridge*, vol. 30, no. 3–4, Fall/Winter 2000. www.nae.edu/File.aspx?id=7327.

"A Sun in a Bottle"

"Fusion power has long been the Holy Grail of energy production, since it offers the possibility of abundant, clean electricity."

—Tom Clynes, author of *The Boy Who Played with Fusion*

Tom Clynes, *The Boy Who Played with Fusion*. New York: Houghton Mifflin Harcourt, 2015, p. 102.

Stars pepper the night sky, their light reaching Earth from nearly unimaginable distances. Many of these stars have burned for hundreds of millions or even billions of years. The sun is about 4.6 billion years old and should shine for another 5 billion years. Its light helped make conditions right on Earth for life to form and thrive, and sunlight continues to power nature today. Plants convert sunlight into the energy they need to grow, and the animals who eat plants use this energy once again, sending it on up the food chain. The remains of ancient plants and microscopic animals, compressed and heated over the ages, became coal, oil, and gas. People rely on these fossil fuels—which are essentially stored sunlight—to run cars, light homes, and power factories. In a sense the sun powers all of life on Earth. But what powers the sun?

The answer is fusion. The force of gravity squeezes all the matter in a star together, keeping the center at an extremely high pressure and incredibly hot temperature. Under these conditions, atoms that would normally repel each other start to slam together and fuse, creating new elements in the process. With each fusion, a burst of energy gets released and radiates outward. Some of the energy reaches Earth and other planets. This energy also helps keep the star from collapsing under its own gravity. A star can continuously produce energy through fusion for billions of years.

Now imagine trying to re-create a massive, scorching star in a laboratory on Earth. This is the challenge facing fusion scientists. Obviously, they cannot literally make a star on Earth—it would swallow up the whole planet. But they can try to mimic the conditions inside a star. This involves using lasers, magnets, vacuum chambers, and other high-tech equipment to create incredibly high temperatures and pressures and then maintain those conditions. Michael Williams of Princeton University says, "Fusion is an expensive science, because you're trying to build a sun in a bottle."[1]

Physicists and engineers have been working on the problem of producing fusion energy on Earth for almost a century, since scientists first figured out in the 1920s and 1930s that fusion was the process powering the sun. Scientists quickly realized that fusion had the potential to provide nearly endless energy, but the path to harnessing this energy has been a long, rocky one.

Though many scientists around the world have achieved fusion reactions with a variety of devices, the world has yet to welcome its first working fusion power plant.

Time Is Running Out ■

Humanity's appetite for energy increases every year. From the gasoline and other fuels that run cars, trucks, and airplanes to the electricity powering people's homes, energy is in high demand. At the same time, current methods of energy production and consumption threaten to destroy the environment and climate. Fossil fuels still provide 87 percent of the world's energy needs, according to a 2015 report from the oil and gas company BP. Yet mining, transporting, and burning these fuels releases harmful pollution into the air, water, and ground. In addition, using fossil fuels for energy puts gases, including carbon dioxide and methane, into the air. These gases trap heat in the atmosphere, contributing to climate change.

Over time, climate change is leading to warmer temperatures around the globe. As a result, sea levels are rising and starting to force people living on islands or in coastal areas out of their homes. Violent storms are becoming more common. Many animals will have to migrate, adapt, or go extinct. Farmers may encounter new pests or diseases that impact their crops. Many of these consequences of climate change are difficult to predict,

A coal-burning power plant fills the sky with pollution. Burning fossil fuels, which still supply 87 percent of the world's energy, threatens to destroy the environment.

and their severity depends on whether people find ways to reduce carbon emissions.

While humanity is already locked into some climate change, thanks to a long history of burning fossil fuels, scientists predict that switching to other means of producing energy could limit the harmful impacts of climate change. But the switch to new energy sources has to happen soon. According a 2014 report from the Intergovernmental Panel on Climate Change, most of the world's electricity must be delivered by low-carbon sources by 2050 in order to keep average global temperatures from rising by any more than 3.6°F (2°C).

Cleaner, Safer Energy ■

The most common energy sources touted as alternatives to fossil fuels are the renewables: solar energy, wind energy, geothermal energy, and hydropower. All are excellent prospects, and development of each is increasing at a steady pace—but not quickly enough to replace fossil fuels anytime soon. Energy from nuclear fission is another important alternative to fossil fuels. Nuclear fission energy, typically abbreviated as just *nuclear energy*, does not contribute to climate change. It currently provides 4 percent of the world's energy needs but could provide much more.

The main problem with nuclear power is that many people fear it. First of all, nuclear power plants produce small amounts of highly hazardous radioactive waste. This waste must be stored very carefully for hundreds of thousands of years. Exposure can be deadly or lead to cancer. As a result of the radioactive fuel and waste stored at nuclear power plants, disasters there can be very dangerous. If the nuclear reaction gets out of control, it can melt the reactor, releasing radioactive materials into the environment. This type of meltdown has happened before, most famously at the Chernobyl power plant in Ukraine in 1986. And in 2011 an earthquake and tsunami damaged part of Japan's Fukushima Daiichi nuclear plant, releasing radioactive materials. Finally, the technology needed to build, maintain, and fuel a nuclear power plant can also be used to make nuclear weapons. Physicist Steven Cowley says, "The world needs a technology that can be switched on within a few decades, and preferably a lot sooner. One that's compatible with current power grids, affordable, nonpolluting, and impossible to use to make nuclear weapons."[2]

WORDS IN CONTEXT

fission

the process of splitting apart the nucleus of an atom

Fusion could be the answer. A nuclear fusion power plant would be much safer than a fission plant. The fusion reaction cannot run out of control, and the radioactive materials involved in fusion are much safer to handle than the ones needed for fission. In addition, fusion would not pollute the environment or worsen climate change. Plus, the main fuel for fusion—deuterium—is found in seawater, one of the most plentiful resources on the planet. Each new experimental fusion reactor and each year of research brings humanity a bit closer to the goal of building a sun in a bottle, a star that could shine right here on Earth and provide energy long into the future.

CHAPTER 1

CURRENT STATUS:
Nuclear Energy

"I started out with a dream to make a 'star in a jar,' a star in my garage, and I ended up meeting the president and developing things that I think can change the world."

—Taylor Wilson, nuclear physicist and child prodigy

Quoted in Taylor Wilson, "Yup, I Built a Nuclear Fusion Reactor," transcript, TED, March 2012. www.ted.com.

Purple sparks dance around a glowing orb. Taylor Wilson, a teenage nuclear physicist, stands behind a wall of lead, meant to protect him from radiation, and stares at the beautiful sight on a video screen. "There it is," he says. "The birth of a star."[3] That glowing purple orb is made of a gas heated to hundreds of millions of degrees. At this temperature, it has reached a new phase of matter and become a plasma. In its depths, atoms are slamming together with such force that some of them join to make new elements. When Wilson successfully produced this fusion reaction for the first time in 2008, he was just fourteen years old, the youngest person ever to achieve fusion.

Creating and Destroying Elements ■
Fusion science is a branch of nuclear physics, a discipline that deals with the particles at the center, or nucleus, of an atom. These particles are called protons and neutrons, and they give an atom its identity. Each element on the periodic table has a unique number of protons in its nucleus. Hydrogen has one; oxygen has eight. The number of neutrons, on the other hand, is variable. Atoms with the same number of protons but different numbers of neutrons are called isotopes. For example, a regular hydrogen atom has no neutrons, while deuterium, a common isotope of

hydrogen, has one neutron, and tritium, hydrogen's only other isotope, has two. Deuterium and tritium also happen to be the most promising fuels for use in fusion reactions on Earth.

The types of energy reactions people encounter in normal life are almost always chemical reactions. For example, in a blazing campfire, elements recombine into new compounds, but they are never created or destroyed. A fire seems to destroy its fuel, but actually the heat of the fire forces compounds inside the wood to react with oxygen in the air, releasing gases and other residue. The original atoms in the wood and air are all still there, only in new arrangements.

Nuclear reactions, on the other hand, alter the composition of the nucleus, often turning one element into another. Inside the sun, hydrogen atoms, which each contain one proton, fuse together to form a helium atom with two protons in its nucleus. Wilson's machine, called a fusor, combines deuterium atoms with other deuterium atoms, also producing helium. Nuclear reactions can also break atoms apart in a process called fission.

Fission reactions are at the heart of all nuclear weapons and all nuclear power plants in the world today. The most common fission reactions use neutrons to break apart the heavy metals uranium or plutonium. When hit with a neutron with sufficient force, the uranium isotope U-235 breaks into lighter elements, such as barium and krypton. This fission releases more neutrons as well as a lot of energy. Inside the reactor at a nuclear power plant, those newly produced neutrons trigger more fissions in a chain reaction. The chain reaction is kept under control with materials that absorb neutrons. The energy released by these fission reactions heats water surrounding the reactor core, and that hot water becomes steam that is used to turn turbines and generate electricity.

Fission reactions are most effective with very heavy atoms, while fusion is most effective with very light atoms, typically hydrogen and its isotopes. In both types of nuclear reactions, some of the mass of the original atoms turns into energy. Einstein's famous formula, $E = mc^2$, describes the relationship between mass

Nuclear power plant workers change out the fuel rods in a reactor. All nuclear power plants currently use fission, the splitting of heavy, radioactive atoms, which creates heat that turns water into steam to turn turbines that generate electricity.

and energy. Basically, it says that a very tiny amount of mass corresponds to a huge amount of energy. As a result, nuclear reactions can turn very small amounts of fuel into vast amounts of energy.

The Case for Fusion ■

Both fission and fusion reactions yield millions of times more energy than the chemical reactions that release energy when coal or oil burn. While 2.2 pounds (1 kg) of coal yields just 12 kilowatt-hours (kWh) of electrical energy—enough to power one lightbulb in an average home for a month—the same amount of refined uranium fission fuel produces 24 million kWh, and 2.2 pounds (1 kg) of deuterium-tritium fusion fuel has the potential to provide 30 million kWh. Thirty million kWh is enough to keep the lights on, all devices charged, and appliances humming along in two thousand to three thousand average American homes for an entire year.

Both fission and fusion produce comparable amounts of energy without worsening climate change. However, fusion offers several advantages over fission. First of all, fusion is safer. Fission involves a chain reaction that can potentially run out of control, while fusion happens only at very high pressure and temperature, conditions that are difficult to maintain. In a disaster these conditions would be lost, fusion would cease, and the reactor would cool. "The thing about fusion is that it is so hard to do, that if you mess up, it turns off,"[4] says David Kirtley, chief executive officer of Helion Energy, a company working on engineering a fusion device.

Secondly, fusion fuels are easy to obtain. While the uranium and plutonium required for fission are limited resources, deuterium and tritium are both plentiful. Deuterium occurs naturally in all water, including seawater. Five gallons (19 L) of seawater contain about 1/8 teaspoon (0.62 mL) of water molecules that contain deuterium atoms. These molecules can be separated out of the rest of the water to produce heavy water, or water that contains a much higher concentration of deuterium than normal. Tritium can be easily produced from lithium, a metal commonly used in some batteries.

Finally, the levels of radioactivity in a fusion plant's operations are much lower and easier to manage than those of a fission plant. While tritium is radioactive, its radiation is too weak to penetrate human skin. It is only considered hazardous if large amounts get into water or food. Plus, a fusion power plant would not actually need to receive shipments of dangerous tritium fuel. Plant operators would instead place a layer of lithium around the reactor. Some of the particles from fusion reactions in the plasma would bombard this lithium, splitting it into tritium and helium. Then the tritium would be collected and fed into the plasma. This process is called tritium breeding.

A fusion plant would produce some radioactive waste. For example, the walls enclosing a fusion chamber become radioactive over time, thanks to bombardment by particles produced during fusion. However, a careful choice of materials for these walls would ensure that this waste is only hazardous for about a century or less. Some of the waste from conventional nuclear fission reactors must be safeguarded for hundreds of thousands of years. "In a fission power plant we create a lot of radioactive waste which lasts for a very long time," says Saskia Mordijck, a fusion scientist at the College of William & Mary in Williamsburg, Virginia. "Whereas in a fusion power plant, the lifetime of this waste is very short. After 50 to 100 years, it will be completely gone and it will not be more radioactive than the surrounding environment and it won't be able to contaminate anything."[5]

The biggest downside of fusion is that it does not work yet as an energy source. Ideally, the fusion reactions inside the reactor would heat the plasma enough for fusion to continue on its own. Current fusion devices use up more power heating and controlling plasma than they generate from fusion reactions. Plus these devices are quite expensive to build and maintain. But once the science is perfected, the cost to build and run a fusion plant should be comparable to the cost of a fission plant.

Many scientists and policy makers believe that the clean, safe, abundant energy fusion could provide justifies the large amounts of money and time spent now on research. However, the time and money keep piling up. Almost an entire century has passed since scientists first realized fusion was a potential source of energy.

Taming Plasma ■
In 1932 Ernest Rutherford, a famous New Zealand physicist considered to be the founder of nuclear physics, and Australian physicist Mark Oliphant demonstrated the world's first fusion reaction in the laboratory. They used a particle accelerator (a machine that speeds up atoms, protons, neutrons, and electrons) to fire deuterium atoms at each other. Occasionally, when the atoms fused, the collision would produce a lot more energy than the atoms had started with. However, this happened very rarely, only once out of every 100 million tries. At the time, Rutherford said that it was ridiculous to think that nuclear reactions would ever provide people

Weapons of Mass Destruction

Nuclear energy has a dark side. The most devastating weapons known to humanity rely on fission and fusion reactions. Conventional atomic bombs get their explosive power from a fission chain reaction. After the United States dropped two of these bombs on Japan at the end of World War II, killing over two hundred thousand civilians, the United States and the Soviet Union raced to develop even more powerful weapons. The result was the hydrogen bomb, also called a thermonuclear weapon. This bomb uses a fission chain reaction to heat and compress a pellet of fusion fuel, igniting a secondary explosion. A thermonuclear bomb is hundreds to thousands of times more powerful than an atomic bomb. Neutron bombs also combine fission and fusion, but they do not produce nearly as much heat or blast damage. Rather, neutron bombs release lethal doses of radiation to a specific area.

Scientists who understood the potential of the hydrogen bomb tried to stop its construction. In 1949 physicists Enrico Fermi and Isidor Rabi wrote the following objection: "The fact that no limits exist to the destructiveness of this weapon makes its very existence and the knowledge of its construction a danger to humanity as a whole. It is necessarily an evil thing considered in any light." Today, however, many countries around the world have built and tested thermonuclear weapons.

Enrico Fermi and Isidor Rabi, "Minority Report on the H-Bomb," *Bulletin of the Atomic Scientists*, November 30, 1976, p. 58.

with energy: "Anyone who expects a source of power from the transformation of these atoms is talking moonshine."[6]

Clearly, Rutherford was wrong about nuclear energy in general, since fission has become an important source of power. But he was right to be skeptical about fusion. To actually produce usable energy from fusion, scientists would need to build a device that could reliably fuse huge amounts of deuterium (or some other light atom) in a sustained process. To do this, they would have to figure out how to handle plasma. The reason Rutherford and Oliphant's experiment produced such a low rate of fusion was that the electrons surrounding the nuclei of the atoms got in the way. In a plasma the electrons that normally zip around the nucleus of each atom get separated, leaving behind naked nuclei, called ions. If a plasma is subjected to high enough temperatures and pressures, these ions will zip around with enough energy to slam together and fuse. The hotter and denser the plasma, the more likely these collisions are to occur.

Plasma is actually the most common state of matter in the universe. Stars, nebulae, and interstellar gases are made of plasma.

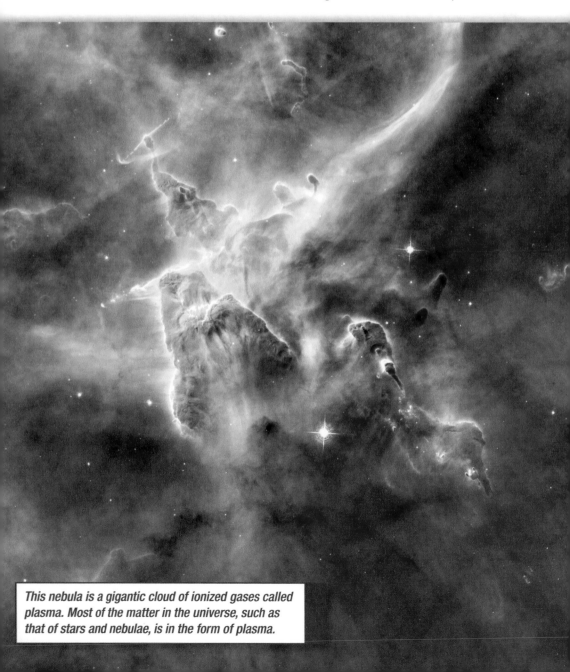

This nebula is a gigantic cloud of ionized gases called plasma. Most of the matter in the universe, such as that of stars and nebulae, is in the form of plasma.

Curing Cancer

Though the goal of most fusion research around the world is energy production, this is just one potential use for fusion. What sparked Taylor Wilson's interest in achieving fusion was not energy, but medicine. Radiation and radioactive isotopes can be used both to diagnose and to treat certain cancers. Medical isotopes currently must be produced using giant particle accelerators, then rushed to hospitals before the unstable isotopes decay. When Wilson was eleven years old, his grandmother was dying from cancer. It bothered the boy that some patients could not get the medical treatment they needed. He realized that the particle accelerators use neutrons to create medical isotopes. He also knew that the deuterium-deuterium fusion reaction gives off neutrons. So he came up with the idea to build a small fusion device that would be able to produce medical isotopes on-site, at a hospital. Though his grandmother passed away from her illness, Wilson hopes that his work will someday help doctors and patients more easily diagnose and treat cancer.

Examples of plasma on Earth include lightning strikes and fluorescent lightbulbs. But not all plasma leads to fusion. For hydrogen fusion to happen on Earth, the plasma must reach 180 million degrees F (100 million degrees C). That is six times hotter than the center of the sun. The sun's advantage is its intense gravity, which exerts enough pressure to produce fusion at a comparatively cool 27 million degrees F (15 million degrees C).

The first experimental fusion energy devices did not produce any fusion reactions at all, and they were not supposed to. Rather, scientists were studying how to control and contain plasma. They knew that the high temperatures needed for fusion would pose a structural challenge. Any solid material such as metal or glass that comes in contact with a 180-million-degree plasma will melt or vaporize.

Thankfully, plasma has an unusual quality: It is a charged field. This is due to the fact that electrons, which have a negative charge, have been separated from protons, which typically have a positive charge. In a normal atom these charges cancel out.

But in a plasma, the separated charges make the field react to electromagnetic forces. In order to build fusion devices, scientists have relied on magnetic fields, electrical currents, lasers, and other tricky methods to contain a hot plasma field without touching it.

The First Fusion Power ■

Many of the most promising fusion devices developed up to this point have used magnetic fields to contain plasma. In 1968 Russian scientists made a breakthrough with a magnetic confinement device they called the tokamak. The name comes from a Russian acronym meaning a donut-shaped chamber with magnetic coils. The tokamak could heat plasma to temperatures ten times higher than other devices. This donut-shaped machine became the model for most fusion devices that followed. Nearly every year from the 1970s through the 1990s, scientists were able to double the amount of fusion power they could produce through larger and larger tokamaks.

WORDS IN
CONTEXT

tokamak

a machine consisting of a donut-shaped tube surrounded by magnets; used to contain hot plasma and harness energy from fusion reactions

Almost all experimental fusion devices operate with one source of fuel: deuterium. It is easier to obtain and safer to handle than radioactive tritium. Leaving out the tritium means that a device can't induce enough fusion reactions to produce power. However, it can still improve other aspects of the fusion process. The researchers often simply estimate the amount of power the device would produce if tritium were included.

Finally, in 1991 researchers at the Joint European Torus (JET) in Culham, England, were ready to demonstrate energy production with deuterium and tritium fuel. JET achieved peak power for two seconds and produced 1.7 megawatts (MW) of power. One MW equals 1,000 kilowatts. That was a small fraction of the power that had to be pumped into the device to get it running. But it was still a milestone in fusion research. The Tokamak Fusion Test Reactor in Princeton, New Jersey, soon achieved similar results. In 1997, JET produced 16 MW of power, a record for power produced from fusion that stands to this day. This is because researchers have been focusing their experimentation on deuterium fuel only, in order to improve and enhance the overall process.

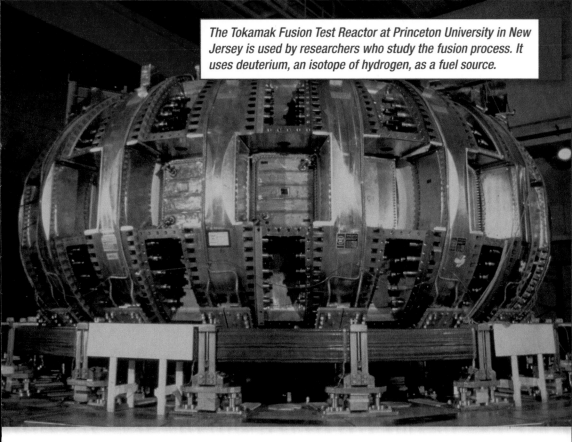

The Tokamak Fusion Test Reactor at Princeton University in New Jersey is used by researchers who study the fusion process. It uses deuterium, an isotope of hydrogen, as a fuel source.

Meanwhile, another sort of fusion device uses giant lasers to quickly compress a tiny pellet of fuel, producing quick bursts of fusion. This is called inertial confinement. While a magnetic confinement device aims to produce a continuously burning plasma, like a campfire, an inertial confinement device works more like a car engine, which runs using a series of small explosions.

The race has been on for either variety of fusion device to surpass breakeven, the point at which the amount of energy that comes out of a fusion reactor equals the amount that was put in. JET used up 24 MW of input power to reach its record-breaking 16 MW peak. Obviously, a fusion power plant will not be of much use to anybody unless it can produce more energy than it consumes.

A Kid Genius ■

By the time Taylor Wilson got interested in nuclear physics in the early 2000s, the science of fusion was well understood. The young science genius started out collecting radioactive materials from antique shops—materials such as radium were once used in clocks, and uranium was once used in glazes for ceramics. "I don't fear radioactivity because I understand it. And that gives me the power to protect myself,"[7] Wilson says.

When Wilson was thirteen, his family moved to Reno, Nevada, so Wilson and his brother could attend the Davidson Academy, a school for gifted children. At age eleven, Wilson had joined the online community Fusor.net, which is devoted to amateur fusion engineering. Through the site, Wilson had struck up friendships with others who had built small fusion devices. At the Davidson Academy, he met new mentors, including the physicist Ronald Phaneuf of the University of Nevada. "He had a depth of understanding I'd never seen in someone that young,"[8] says Phaneuf, who gave Wilson permission to build a fusion reactor in his lab. Phaneuf felt that would be safer than allowing Wilson to keep tinkering in his garage at home.

With the help of his mentors, Wilson assembled the materials he needed for a fusor and got to work building. Two years later, the machine was complete. Since developing that first fusion device, Wilson has won numerous prizes in national and international science fairs. In 2012 he met President Barack Obama to present a project aimed at countering terrorism with an inexpensive radiation detection device. By 2013 he was working on new designs for fission reactors. "Someone saying it can't be done, or it's extremely hard to do, just makes me want to do it," Wilson says. "I just don't accept that I can't. I really do think that someday we'll have fusion power and that I can be part of the breakthrough to make it happen."[9]

Fusion science surely needs more kids—and adults—like Taylor Wilson. Once, many people believed that landing on the moon would be impossible. But US scientists accomplished the feat within a decade of setting the goal, thanks to plentiful funding and a sense that it was vitally important to beat the Soviet Union there. In the minds of many scientists, fusion energy is a much more important goal. But as Wilson's mentor Phaneuf has said, "Getting to the moon is almost trivial in comparison to nuclear fusion energy."[10] The history of fusion energy has been one of slow, incremental progress. Some wonder how many more years of research and how many more billions of dollars it will take. It is not clear whether humans will harness fusion energy in time to make a difference in the fight against climate change.

CHAPTER 2

PROBLEMS: Breaking Even and Scaling Up

"There's unlikely to be a eureka moment but one day the operators of [the International Thermonuclear Experimental Reactor], or some other reactor, will get their settings just right, the plasma will get hot, stay hot, and burn like a piece of the sun."

—Daniel Clery, author of *A Piece of the Sun: The Quest for Fusion Energy*

Daniel Clery, *A Piece of the Sun: The Quest for Fusion Energy.* New York and London: Overlook Duckworth, 2013, p. 29.

Getting a couple of atoms to fuse together is not so difficult. After all, scientists first accomplished fusion reactions in 1932. Now anyone—even teens—can download the instructions to build a basic fusion device. The Fusor.net forum keeps a running tally of hobbyists and student groups who have achieved fusion on their own, unaffiliated with official fusion research programs. The list contains sixty-six names and counting. While achieving fusion is not easy by any stretch of the imagination, it is definitely doable. However, turning fusion reactions into a reliable, affordable, and safe source of electrical power remains an unsolved problem.

The main goal of current fusion research is to surpass the breakeven point. Scientists must find a way to get more energy out of a fusion device than goes in. Most likely, to achieve breakeven, the fusion reactor will have to reach ignition, a state in which the fusion reactions themselves provide enough energy to keep fusion going. At this point, the reactor should not need to rely on external electrical power to keep the plasma hot. The process is similar to lighting a fire. At first a person needs to hold a match or lighter beside the fuel. But once the fire starts burning with enough heat, an external source of heat is no longer necessary. Researchers hope that fusion reactors will soon be able to burn continuously as long as fuel is added, just like a furnace. They even refer to a reactor in this state as a burning plasma. Unfortunately, several hurdles remain that prevent reaching either ignition or breakeven.

Hotter than the Sun ■

Three conditions must be met in order for any fusion reactor to produce more energy than it consumes. The device must achieve a high enough temperature as well as a high enough density and must maintain these conditions for a long enough time. The physicist John D. Lawson first defined these criteria in 1957, writing, "These conditions are very severe."[11] In an interview fifty years later, he said, "I knew that I wouldn't see fusion power in my own lifetime, although most people were talking about it coming in 20 years or so. They still are."[12]

WORDS IN
CONTEXT

ignition

in fusion research, the point at which fusion reactions within a reactor produce enough heat to keep fusion going

These three conditions complement each other, meaning that a device that focuses on establishing one condition does not have to be quite as successful in the others. In order to surpass breakeven, the three values multiplied together, also called the triple product, must be higher than a certain number. The two main approaches to fusion energy—magnetic confinement and inertial confinement—focus on maximizing different combinations of these conditions. Inertial confinement fusion devices produce much higher density than magnetic confinement devices for an extremely brief amount of time. Magnetic confinement devices operate at a lower density but aim to keep the plasma confined for a longer period. Temperatures in the two approaches are comparable, since temperature must be above a certain level in order for fusion to occur.

For a deuterium-tritium fusion reaction to surpass breakeven, the fuel must reach a temperature of over 180 million degrees F (100 million degrees C), six times hotter than the center of the sun. Temperatures this high are nearly impossible

A candle will continue to burn on its own once it is lit by an external heat source, and getting the fusion process to continue on its own after an initial ignition is the goal of fusion-energy researchers.

to imagine, let alone create in a laboratory. Water boils at 212°F (100°C), and stainless steel melts at 2,750°F (1,510°C). If a normal thermometer went up into the hundreds of millions of degrees, it would have to be almost 250 miles (402 km) long. At a temperature this high, any material evaporates. To reach such blistering heat, magnetic confinement fusion devices use a combination of several different heating techniques that include electrical currents, known as ohmic heating, and beams of very energetic particles, called neutral beam injection. Inertial confinement devices use lasers to compress and heat fusion fuel very quickly.

In the 1990s the Tokamak Fusion Test Reactor in Princeton set a temperature record when its plasma reached 918 million degrees F (510 million degrees C). But the entire plasma does not get this hot. The plasma within a fusion reactor is hottest in the middle, while the edges are much cooler. Energy and particles continually leak out from the edges. Engineers do their best to design fusion devices that keep these heat losses to a minimum.

Under Pressure ■

The second condition required for breakeven is a certain density. As the plasma heats up, its particles move faster and faster, expanding with increasing force. If nothing kept the plasma together, it would fly apart in all directions, dissipating its energy and heat into the surroundings. A fusion device must keep the energetic plasma particles close enough together that they are likely to collide and fuse. The density required in a magnetic confinement device is about one-millionth that of air. That does not seem like much, but even this relatively low density is difficult to maintain at such blistering temperatures.

Density and temperature multiplied together equal pressure, so often fusion scientists talk about achievements in pressure rather than density or temperature separately. As pressure increases in a fusion device, many more fusion reactions occur, but

Chaos Science

In a chaotic system such as a plasma, very tiny changes in the conditions in a small area tend to escalate and alter the state of the whole system. The most familiar chaotic system is the weather. When Edward Lorenz of MIT first proposed chaos theory, he used a memorable example to describe how the science worked. He said that if a butterfly flapped its wings in Brazil, this could lead to a tornado in Texas. Tiny changes in movement, temperature, or humidity of the air in a small area can grow into entire weather systems. This is now known as the butterfly effect. As a result of this effect, the weather is very difficult to predict, especially in the town-sized areas and day-by-day time scales that humans care about. The stock market is another chaotic system. Small changes in spending or saving can result in big leaps in stock prices. It is no wonder weather reports and stock market predictions are so often incorrect.

Flowing water has a chaotic behavior known as turbulence. The faster water flows, the more unpredictable its motion gets. The water coming out of a faucet turned on full blast tends to shiver and shake rather than move in a smooth column. Plasma can also exhibit turbulence, making it very difficult to control or predict its flow.

heat escapes more rapidly. Most magnetic confinement fusion devices operate at pressures comparable to that of the weight of air at sea level, called one atmosphere. The Alcator C-Mod tokamak nuclear fusion reactor at the Massachusetts Institute of Technology (MIT), now out of commission, set successive records for highest pressure in a magnetic confinement fusion device. One of these records occurred on its last day of operation in 2016, when it reached over two atmospheres of pressure.

An inertial confinement device, in contrast, reaches billions of atmospheres in pressure. But it cannot maintain this pressure for very long. The fusion device at the National Ignition Facility (NIF) at the Lawrence Livermore National Laboratory (LLNL) in California has achieved 150 billion atmospheres' worth of pressure but only for 150 trillionths of a second.

An inertial confinement device can afford to skimp on time because it exerts such high pressures. However, magnetic confinement devices must maintain pressure for as long as possible. Called confinement time, this third and final condition measures how quickly the device loses energy. Think of what happens to a house in the winter when the heat is switched off. Gradually, the house will cool. A house that is well insulated will lose heat more slowly than one with open windows. Fusion devices try to be more like the well-insulated house. They aim to lose heat as slowly as possible by building in safeguards to keep leaks to a minimum. Once too much heat is lost, fusion will cease. Most current devices can only maintain fusion conditions for seconds or minutes at a time. However, a reactor built by the company Tokamak Energy in the United Kingdom has sustained a plasma for twenty-nine hours.

WORDS IN CONTEXT
confinement time
the amount of time a fusion device can maintain a certain temperature without losing so much heat that fusion ceases

The Plasma Puzzle ■

Many of the problems that fusion scientists and engineers encounter while trying to increase density, temperature, or confinement time involve plasma. It is a perplexing, tricky substance to work with, as its behavior tends to be chaotic and difficult to predict.

"Controlling a plasma in a fusion device is not an easy thing to do. It's a bit like trying to keep a jelly still in your hand,"[13] says Andrew Kirk of the Culham Centre for Fusion Energy.

In early experiments with magnetic confinement and high-temperature plasma, scientists noted that plasma tended to lose heat rapidly, writhe in its prison, or even suddenly collapse, losing all its energy. They called these plasma problems instabilities. One instability causes the central temperature in the plasma to rise steadily, then drop suddenly, then rise again. This instability is called sawteeth because a graph of the temperature changes looks like a row of jagged teeth. Another variety, called an edge-localized mode, or ELM, is similar to a solar flare—an eruption that occurs on the surface of the sun. In an ELM the plasma suddenly expels a burst of particles toward the wall of the device, leading to huge heat losses and potentially damaging the wall.

The worst sort of instability, though, is a disruption. In a disruption the flow of electrical current through the plasma sud-

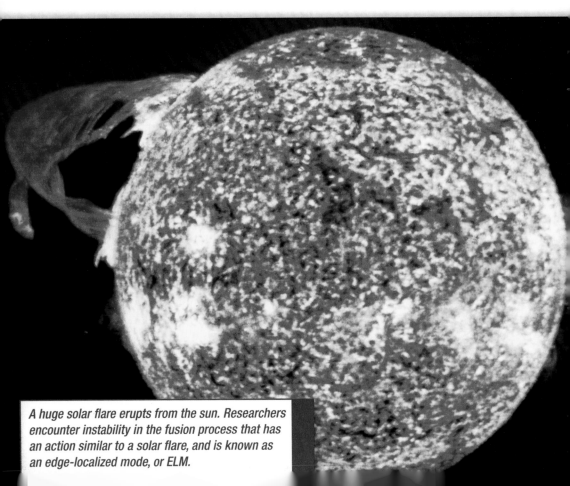

A huge solar flare erupts from the sun. Researchers encounter instability in the fusion process that has an action similar to a solar flare, and is known as an edge-localized mode, or ELM.

Impurities

Ideally, the plasma in a fusion device contains nothing but deuterium and tritium nuclei, zipping around at maddening speeds and smacking into each other to produce lots of energy. But in reality, the plasma cannot remain pristine. First of all, each fusion reaction produces helium. These helium atoms have nowhere to go, so they remain in the plasma, contaminating it with so-called helium ash that builds up over time. In addition, in a magnetic confinement device, the hot plasma is kept suspended inside a vacuum chamber. While the bulk of the plasma never touches the walls of the chamber, some particles inevitably escape and slam into the wall, knocking off atoms of whatever elements happen to be there. These wayward atoms are known as impurities, and they can cause the reactor to lose precious heat. Even a very small level of certain impurities can prevent the device from ever being able to reach ignition. Researchers have yet to find a material for the walls of a reactor that will not introduce harmful impurities. But they have come up with a work-around: a diverter. This is a device that acts like a filter to clean impurities out of the plasma.

denly ceases, leading to a sudden drop in temperature. This releases all of the formerly contained energetic particles, which smack into the walls of the fusion device, potentially damaging important components. In a way a disruption is like popping a balloon. It is sudden, violent, and depletes all pressure in the system. Thankfully, engineers can see a disruption coming and take steps to reduce the damage. Larry Baylor of Oak Ridge National Laboratory says, "A disruption occurs when the plasma becomes unstable and starts to move uncontrollably. You have to cool the plasma down quickly so that it does not hit the wall with that thermal energy."[14]

Instabilities affect inertial confinement fusion as well. In this case instabilities in plasma may make the pellet of fuel fly apart before it is compressed to a pressure high enough to kick off fusion. Researchers get better at wrangling plasma with each passing year. But the science remains sheathed in mystery. "Advances in plasma physics mean that we are beginning to understand a lot more about how it behaves, but there is still much that we don't know—it's a fascinating branch of science,"[15] says Kirk.

Paying the Price ■

Experimental devices have proved that it is scientifically feasible to produce energy from fusion. Over the years, each new device has pushed at least one of the three conditions closer to the goals of breakeven and ignition. There is every reason to believe that new experimental devices will succeed in achieving these goals. Many in the fusion community have placed their hopes in the International Thermonuclear Experimental Reactor (ITER), a gigantic magnetic confinement reactor currently being constructed in France. "We have waited 60 years to get close to controlled fusion—we are now close in both magnetic and inertial," says Steven Cowley of the Culham Centre for Fusion Energy. "We must keep at it."[16]

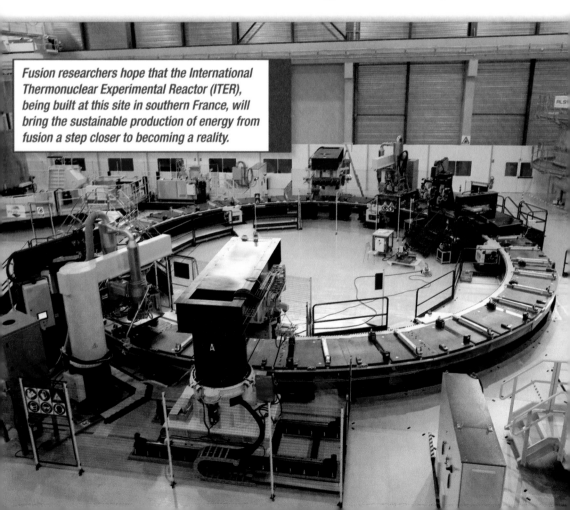

Fusion researchers hope that the International Thermonuclear Experimental Reactor (ITER), being built at this site in southern France, will bring the sustainable production of energy from fusion a step closer to becoming a reality.

However, in order to move from experiment to a full-scale power plant, researchers need money.

Some fusion scientists believe that working fusion power plants would have been possible as early as 2000 if researchers had had adequate funding. Finding money for fusion research continues to be a vexing problem. "It's expensive research that can only be done at large scales," says Cowley, "and nobody sees the need right now. Every time there's talk about climate change, funding goes up for a while."[17] The availability of funding for fusion is also related to the cost of other sources of energy. When coal, gas, or oil prices rise, governments are more likely to invest in alternative energy sources such as fusion. When fossil fuel prices drop, funding for alternative energy does, too.

Cowley goes on to say that his team knows how to make fusion energy a reality. They just do not have the resources it would take to get the job done. "For $20 billion in cash, I could build you a working reactor," he says. "It would be big, and maybe not very reliable, but 25 years ago we didn't even know if we'd be able to make fusion work. Now, the only question is whether we'll be able to make it affordable."[18]

CHAPTER 3

SOLUTIONS:
Zap It with Lasers

"In laser fusion, an ignited target is like a miniature star of about a 10th of a millimeter, which produces the energy equivalent of a few gallons of gasoline over a fraction of a billionth of a second. We are not there yet, but we are making progress."

—Riccardo Betti, Laboratory for Laser Energetics

Quoted in University of Rochester, "A First for Direct-Drive Fusion," September 6, 2016. www.rochester.edu.

In less than a billionth of a second, 192 laser blasts converged on a minuscule gold cylinder the size of a pencil eraser. The cylinder exploded, compressing an even tinier pellet of fusion fuel inside. That fuel gave off energy—twice as much energy as the lasers had imparted. This fusion breakthrough happened in 2013 at the NIF in California. Riccardo Betti of the University of Rochester, who was not involved in the experiment, said, "If fusion will ever become a viable source of energy, we may look back and say that in 2013, for the first time, a plasma produced more energy out than it took in."[19]

Though a remarkable achievement, the NIF still had not reached ignition or even breakeven. Though the fusion fuel gave off more energy than it took in from the lasers, just 0.5 percent of the total laser energy actually reached the fuel. Most of it zipped past. Overall, the experiment still used up more power than it generated. The energy the fusion reactions produced was only enough to keep a 60-watt bulb lit for five minutes. It took about one hundred times more energy than that to prepare the chamber, power the lasers, and do everything else necessary to run the experiment.

Yet this was still an important milestone for fusion. "This is closer than anyone's gotten before," said Omar Hurricane, a physicist at the LLNL and the lead author of the study. "Our theoretical understanding is that if we keep pushing in this direction we have a chance, but we can't really promise one way or the other. We can't honestly tell you when we will get ignition. We are working like mad to go in that direction."[20]

Explosion, Implosion, Fusion ■

Laser fusion, a simple term for inertial confinement fusion using lasers, occurs in a series of steps that all take place within that mere billionth of a second. The key components are a bunch of high-powered lasers and a tiny pellet of fusion fuel, about the size of a single peppercorn. The pellet typically contains a frozen mix of deuterium and tritium fuel, held together inside a coating made of silicon and plastic. First, multiple powerful laser beams all focus their energy on the pellet of fuel at the same time, heating it evenly from all directions.

WORDS IN CONTEXT

inertia

the tendency of an object to resist a change in its motion

The heat burns off the pellet's coating, which explodes outward. The laws of physics state that every action has an equal and opposite reaction. This outward explosive force presses inward on the fuel at the center of the pellet, creating an implosion. This inward force is one hundred times greater than the thrust required to launch a rocket ship into space. It exerts pressure hundreds of billions of times greater than the weight of the atmosphere. But the pellet cannot blast off like a rocket, because the thrust comes evenly from all directions at once. Instead, it must shrink into a tighter and tighter space. "When the lasers are fired, the capsule is compressed 35 times. That is like compressing a basketball to the size of a pea,"[21] says Debbie Callahan of LLNL. As the pellet shrinks in size, its temperature and density greatly increase, forcing the solid pellet to become a plasma. The greatest temperature and pressure are exerted on the atoms at the very center of the pellet. It is here in the center that fusion reactions begin to occur.

Finally, if a high enough temperature and density have been reached, fusion reactions spread outward from the center, creating a burning plasma. At the same time, the pellet starts to

A photo captures the first hydrogen bomb test in 1952. Scientists at that time began to consider whether the fusion of hydrogen atoms used in the bomb might also be used to create electricity.

expand and cool again. However, thanks to inertia, or the tendency of an object to resist a change in its motion, the fusion reactions spread faster than the expansion. Ideally, all of the fuel fuses before its density and temperature drop back down. The fact that inertia keeps the fusion fuel close together in the instant after compression leads to the name *inertial confinement fusion*.

The minuscule pellets used at the NIF each have the potential to release about as much energy as burning a barrel of oil—if all the fuel fuses. That amount of energy could keep a 60-watt bulb lit for over two weeks. In an inertial confinement power plant, these tiny pellets would explode one after another, providing a nearly continuous supply of energy. This is analogous to the workings of a car's engine, which uses successive explosions of small amounts of gasoline to push pistons down again and again. In a car this motion turns the wheels. In a fusion power plant, the energy produced in each explosion would likely heat water in order to produce steam to turn turbines.

A Miniature Nuclear Bomb ■

Inertial confinement fusion has a lot in common with the hydrogen bomb, which owes its destructive power to a combination of fission and fusion reactions. In these bombs, also called thermonuclear weapons, a fission explosion compresses and heats a layer of fusion fuel, which then also explodes. These reactions produce hundreds or even thousands of times more destructive power than a fission-only nuclear bomb. A hydrogen bomb easily surpasses breakeven, releasing much more energy than is required to set off the reaction. It also reaches ignition and burns through all of its fusion fuel. The trouble is that this energy is not very useful. The bomb obliterates its surroundings, destroying anything or anyone within an area of about 30 miles (48 km). Inertial confinement fusion is an attempt to tame such a bomb and make it useful. Instead of a devastating blast, fusion engineers aim to produce small explosions that will not destroy anything but will still produce usable energy.

The LLNL in California once focused on the design of nuclear weapons. A few years after the first successful test of a hydrogen bomb in 1952, scientists there started wondering whether a hydrogen-bomb-like device might be able to provide electricity. One young physicist was even tasked with figuring out whether it might make sense to hollow out a mountain, fill it with steam, and then set off a hydrogen bomb inside. The idea was that the explosion would expel the steam to turn turbines and generate electricity. Unfortunately, the mountain probably would not survive many such explosions. In the end the far-fetched idea was abandoned.

But some scientists imagined setting off smaller, controlled fusion explosions in order to produce energy. To do this, they would need something other than a destructive fission explosion in order to quickly compress and heat the fusion fuel. The answer they needed was invented in 1960: the laser. As laser technology advanced, it became clear that these narrow, high-energy beams of light could provide the right kind of power. One of the benefits is that the source of the laser light can be situated at a distance from its target. Thus, the laser machinery is protected from the mini explosions used to initiate fusion.

Welcome to *Star Trek* ■

The NIF at LLNL opened in 2009 after twelve years of construction. Three football fields would fit inside the main building, which houses the world's largest and most precise laser system. Forty thousand optical instruments help guide, amplify, and focus up to 192 laser beams.

These beams shine into a 33-foot-wide (10-m) metal sphere called the target chamber, which is studded with equipment to track and measure the results of experiments. It is an awe-inspiring sight straight out of a science fiction story. Fittingly, the target chamber actually appeared in the 2013 movie *Star Trek into Darkness*. The engine room of the starship *Enterprise* in the movie is actually the target chamber at the NIF. During a fusion experiment, the fuel pellet sits at the very center of the target

A fuel pellet is shown here inside a hohlraum. The gold of the hohlraum walls create X-rays when heated with lasers, and the X-rays ignite the pellet to initiate the fusion process.

A Drop of Liquid

In laser fusion the shape of the pellet of fuel matters a lot. The more perfect its shape, the more even the implosion. Most pellets contain solid, frozen fuel encased in a mixture of plastic and metal. However, it is pretty much impossible to craft a perfect sphere out of a solid material. In 2016 researchers at the NIF tried something new. They used liquid fuel instead. In a vacuum a liquid forms a perfectly spherical droplet.

The researchers still needed to use that plastic and metal shell, though—the force of the shell burning off is what causes the fuel to implode. But a liquid droplet would not hold its shape inside metal. It would drip or freeze. So the researchers separated the liquid from its shell with a layer of foam.

During the first series of experiments with the liquid fuel, researchers fired the NIF's lasers at reduced power. Even at low power, they saw close to the same number of neutrons as had been generated with solid fuel and high-powered lasers. The number of neutrons produced correlates to the number of fusion reactions. Future research will prove whether the liquid fuel approach will work when the power gets turned up.

chamber, and all of the air gets sucked out to create a vacuum. The chamber also helps shield the rest of the facility and the people working there from radiation produced during experiments. During the groundbreaking ceremony for the NIF in 1997, the energy secretary of the United States at the time, Federico Peña, said, "NIF will unleash the power of the heavens to make Earth a better place."[22] The goal of the facility is right there in its name: ignition. Though the NIF hosts a range of scientific research, its primary focus is fusion energy.

A Better Way to Squeeze Jell-O ∎

Inertial confinement fusion will have to reach the perfect combination of three factors—density, temperature, and time—in order to reach fusion. Inertial confinement focuses mainly on producing incredibly high density. The point of constructing such a huge laser system at the NIF was to increase the amount of laser power researchers had available. They thought more power would lead to greater density as the fuel imploded.

However, it turns out that plasma does not like being squished. As the laser power was cranked up, tiny inconsistencies in the spherical shape of the fuel pellet seemed to matter more and more. If a tiny spot experienced just a little less pressure than its surroundings, the plasma would bulge out there and escape, ruining the implosion before fusion had a chance to get going. E. Michael Campbell of the Laboratory for Laser Energetics at the University of Rochester in New York, a facility that performs inertial fusion research, explains the problem: "It's like squeezing a balloon with your hands," he says. "There are always parts that pop out where your hands aren't."[23] Richard Petrasso of the Plasma Science and Fusion Center at MIT uses Jell-O as an example. Imagine trying to squeeze a handful of Jell-O as tightly as possible, he says, "without any of [it] squeezing out between your fingers."[24] Scientists try to shape the pellet perfectly and then compress the surface as evenly as possible, but tiny imperfections always sneak in.

The NIF came up with an innovative way to maintain a more uniform pressure on the pellet. Researchers housed the fuel pellet inside a slightly larger, cylindrical capsule called the hohlraum, which is typically made of gold or another heavy metal. Rather than shining directly onto the pellet, the laser beams shine through holes at the two ends of the gold capsule and onto the interior walls of the capsule. The innermost layer of the gold wall evaporates, becoming a dense metal plasma full of X-rays that bounce around like light in a room full of mirrors. This rapidly and evenly heats the pellet until it implodes.

The hohlraum design, also called indirect drive, helped the NIF team achieve its 2013 breakthrough. But much work remains to be done. Hurricane and his team must double the pressure exerted on the fuel pellet in order to achieve ignition. That means they need to compress it even faster while keeping the shape of the compression perfectly even. The solution may require finding a new coating for the pellet, one that will help it compress more effectively. Or the researchers may find that an egg-shaped hohlraum works better than a cylinder. Still, "the biggest limitation right now is laser energy,"[25] according to Hurricane. His team needs more, but they are already using all that they can get with the NIF's system. And the NIF has some of the most advanced equipment in the world.

Fast-Forward to Fast Ignition ■

Though the NIF's equipment is the best for now, other facilities are catching up. They are also performing important research with smaller laser systems. Many of these groups have stuck with direct drive, the original approach that shines laser light directly

---

Laser World Records

First: Invented in 1960 by Theodore Maiman, the first laser used a ruby to turn flashes of regular light into an energetic beam of red light.

Biggest: The laser system at the NIF in California is the world's biggest and most energetic.

Fastest: Very quick laser pulses allow scientists to observe very fast processes, such as moving electrons. The fastest laser pulse clocked in at just sixty-seven attoseconds. An attosecond is a billionth of a billionth of a second. This speed record belongs to Zenghu Chang, a professor at the University of Central Florida.

Most powerful: The LFEX laser at Osaka University produced 2 petawatts of power in a pulse that lasted one-trillionth of a second.

Most hard-working: A super laser named Bivoj after a figure in Czech mythology can sustain 1,000 watts of output. The LFEX can only reach its peak power a few times a day, while Bivoj can fire repeatedly. The laser was developed by the Central Laser Facility in the United Kingdom and HiLASE (high average power pulsed laser) in the Czech Republic.

---

on the fuel. The Laboratory for Laser Energetics uses the OMEGA laser to study the direct-drive approach. The Institute of Laser Engineering at Osaka University in Japan is also experimenting with this method. Researchers there and around the world are interested in a new twist on inertial fusion called fast ignition. Osaka University even named its star machine the Laser for Fast Ignition Experiments (LFEX). In 2015 the LFEX became the most powerful laser ever fired. It produced a 2-petawatt pulse that lasted one-trillionth of a second. Two petawatts is 2 million billion watts.

The fast ignition approach to fusion energy uses two laser bursts instead of one. The first compresses the fuel. The second heats the fuel at the instant of maximum compression. Laser light usually cannot penetrate through the dense plasma formed during the pellet's compression. However, a very intense, very brief laser pulse such as the ones produced by the LFEX may be able to get in. Researchers at Osaka University have also investigated building a special funnel into the fuel pellet to provide a pathway for the heating laser pulse.

Surprisingly, fast ignition actually uses up less energy than regular inertial fusion. Two million billion watts is an incredible amount of power, but power is a measure of energy over time. The laser fires so quickly that it is not actually using up very much energy. A microwave running for two seconds drains as much energy as the 2-petawatt laser firing for one-trillionth of a second. Reducing the energy it takes to run a fusion device is called an energy gain. This makes breakeven more likely because it means the fusion fuel does not have to release quite as much energy to surpass the amount of energy the system uses up.

The Megajoule Laser (LMJ) facility in France is also focusing on fast ignition research. Run by France's Atomic Energy Commission, the LMJ began operations in 2014. This facility is comparable to the NIF in terms of size and scope. However, it also houses a super-powerful laser comparable to the LFEX. PETAL, for PETawatt Aquitaine Laser, can produce 1.2 petawatts of power in an extremely short burst.

The NIF and LMJ may serve as stepping-stones to an even larger facility, dubbed the HiPER project, for High Power laser

An engineer positions the target in France's Megajoule Laser Facility. The facility's super-laser can generate bursts of more than a petawatt (a quadrillion watts) of power onto the target.

Energy Research. HiPER's goal would be to build on accomplishments at current experimental laser fusion facilities in order to demonstrate actual energy production. Limitations with current experimental devices mean that the lasers can only fire once every few hours. A commercial fusion power plant using the laser approach would need to fuse a pellet of fuel at least every ten seconds—this would be one of HiPER's main areas of focus. Though there are no construction plans yet for the facility, the United Kingdom is leading a cooperative effort sponsored by countries in the European Union to conceptualize it.

China is also working on inertial confinement fusion. It has developed a series of laser facilities, dubbed the Shenguang (SG) lasers, each more powerful than the last. Plans are under way for

SG-IV, with the goal of achieving ignition and a burning plasma by 2020. However, given past experiences with fusion research, China's goal may slip out of reach.

A Doomed Quest? ■

When the NIF first opened in 2009, the mood among fusion researchers was optimistic. Computer models and simulations showed that the facility should be able to reach ignition. In fact, researchers expected to achieve ignition by 2012. They hoped to follow up on that accomplishment with a prototype for a fusion power plant. But 2012 came and went with no power plant in sight. "Laser fusion is not even a twinkle in someone's eye at this point,"[26] says Charles Seife, author of the book *Sun in a Bottle: The Strange History of Fusion and the Science of Wishful Thinking*.

Even Omar Hurricane, whose efforts achieved the breakthrough at the NIF in 2013, realizes that a laser fusion power plant is still a distant goal. "It will be a long time before [laser fusion] is practical. It's anyone's guess how long, but years is unrealistically short,"[27] he says. "I actually don't constrain myself personally with the practical applications at this point."[28] He has compared the quest for ignition to climbing a mountain—except the summit is covered with clouds, so no one knows how much farther it is to the top. A 2016 report on the efforts of the NIF said that achieving ignition on the NIF's current equipment was unlikely in the next two years and uncertain over the long term. Rather than pushing toward ignition and an eventual power plant, the facility plans to focus on better understanding the behavior of extremely dense plasma.

The mood surrounding laser fusion may be dark now. A single breakthrough, however, could speed up research and bring the world closer to a fusion energy solution.

CHAPTER 4

SOLUTIONS:
Wrap It with Magnets

"In the late 2020s, ITER will reach fusion burn, pouring out energy like a little star."

—Steven Cowley, director of the Culham Centre for Fusion Energy

Quoted in Culham Centre for Fusion Energy, "How to Reach 200 Million Degrees," 2012. www.ccfe.ac.uk.

At a construction site in Saint-Paul-lès-Durance, France, cranes rise high over the landscape, placing beams and blocks—the skeleton of a new fusion research facility named the International Thermonuclear Experimental Reactor, or ITER. At the heart of the construction site sits a circular opening surrounded by a thick wall that rises higher and higher as construction continues. These are the beginnings of the structure that will house the largest tokamak ever built. It will stand 100 feet (30 m) tall and will weigh 23,000 tons (20,865 metric tons). It will be the most expensive scientific instrument ever built, with an estimated price tag of at least US$20 billion. That is three times as expensive as the Large Hadron Collider, the world's biggest particle accelerator.

ITER's fusion reactor and associated machinery are so gigantic and technically complicated that the first building to appear at the construction site was the Assembly Building. Filled with cranes, hoists, and machining equipment for forming custom components, this building exists in order to construct the rest of the facility. Its mirrored walls reflect the landscape, and a huge banner hanging from one side proudly proclaims: "Bringing the power of the sun to Earth." The acronym ITER has a second meaning as well. The Latin word *iter* means "the way."

Will this new reactor be the way forward for humanity, into a future with clean, boundless energy? Many believe so. The governments of the European Union, China, India, Japan, Korea, Russia, and the United States have all invested in ITER in the hopes that the project will succeed.

However, the project is behind schedule and over budget. The reactor was supposed to be ready to turn on by 2016. Now that date has been pushed back to 2025. That extra time costs a lot of money. Still, the fusion community remains excited about the prospects of the new facility. Computer models show that ITER's giant reactor should be able to soar past breakeven to produce 500 MW of power from 50 MW of input power. Bernard Bigot, director of ITER, says, "If we are successful, it will be a real breakthrough for the energy supply of the world. We are fully committed to deliver."[29]

A Magnetic Cage ■

Plasma is a conductor, meaning that it can carry an electrical current. Just as a wire allows electricity to flow through from one place to another, plasma also allows the flow of electricity. As electricity flows through any conductor, a magnetic field forms around the moving current. If the current is flowing through a straight wire from left to right, the magnetic field would form in a circle around the wire, wrapping from front to back and all around.

If the electrical current is very strong, then the resulting magnetic field will also be very strong—strong enough to squeeze plasma. This is called the pinch effect, and it is at the heart of the design of magnetic confinement fusion devices. The pinch effect can keep hot plasma flowing in a line suspended in space in the middle of a container made of glass or metal. The magnetic field wraps around the hot plasma like a cord wound tightly around a package, forming a cage that can help keep the plasma confined.

If the container holding the suspended plasma is shaped like a cylinder, the plasma would flow through from one end to the other, then escape. It would be impossible to heat it up enough for fusion to occur. As early as 1947, physicists realized that the answer to this problem is simple: Wrap the cylinder around on itself to make a donut. Then the plasma can flow around in a circle inside without hitting the walls.

A tokamak is one of the most promising fusion reactor designs. Inside this device, charged plasma particles flow around the inside of a donut-shaped tube. Magnets placed around the tube form a cage for the plasma. Vertical magnets (blue) cause a magnetic field to flow around the inside of the tube (blue arrow). Horizontal magnets (green) cause a magnetic field to wrap around the walls of the tube (green arrows). These two magnetic fields combine to create one, spiraling field (red arrows). Particles of plasma follow this path as they are heated to the temperature required for fusion to occur.

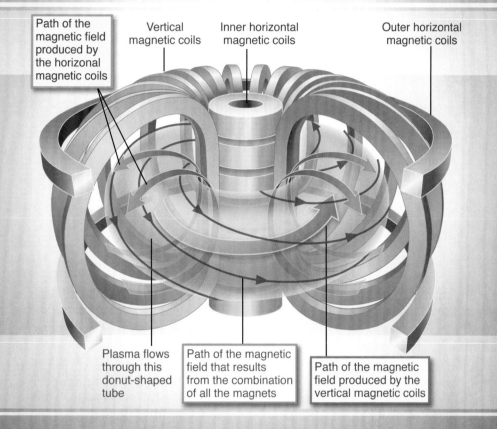

Path of the magnetic field produced by the horizonal magnetic coils

Vertical magnetic coils

Inner horizontal magnetic coils

Outer horizontal magnetic coils

Plasma flows through this donut-shaped tube

Path of the magnetic field that results from the combination of all the magnets

Path of the magnetic field produced by the vertical magnetic coils

Source: Eurofusion Consortium, "Tokamak Principle," September 20, 2011. www.euro-fusion.org.

However, the pinch effect is not strong enough to keep super-hot plasma under control. It tends to leak out and escape. Modern magnetic confinement devices add additional magnets that wrap around the device both horizontally and vertically, making the cage even more secure. Imprisoning plasma with a bunch of crisscrossing magnets is a tricky science. According to one

Electromagnetism

People use electricity every day when they switch on a lightbulb or plug in an electronic device. They encounter magnetism when they stick a photo to the fridge. But they may not realize that these two phenomena are different manifestations of the same underlying force—electromagnetism. The key to understanding magnets and electricity is realizing that all particles carry either a negative or positive charge. Like charges repel each other, while opposite charges attract each other. An electrical current is composed of a series of negatively charged electrons all moving through a wire or other conductor. Any moving charged particle also creates a magnetic field around itself. The magnetic field moves in a direction opposite to the motion of the particle and only exerts a force on other charged particles that happen to be nearby.

The magnetic field produced by a single, straight wire is quite weak. A wire wound tightly around a metal core creates a much stronger magnetic field around itself. This is called an electromagnet. People can make one at home by winding wire around a nail, then generating current through the wire with a battery. The nail will become magnetized. This is basically what happens in a tokamak, although on a much larger scale. A tokamak's magnetic coils are formed from tightly wound wires. They only start generating magnetic fields when fed electric current.

fusion power researcher, physicist Richard Feynman once compared the trick to "trying to hold Jell-O with rubber bands."[30]

The vertically oriented magnets wrap around the outside of the donut-shaped tube where the plasma flows, like large beads on a circular bracelet. These coils create a magnetic field that flows around the center of the donut shape. The field lines are like a highway for the charged particles of the plasma. The donut shape causes a problem, though. The magnetic coils that wrap around are clustered more closely together in the center of the donut and farther apart on the outside. This forms a magnetic field that is stronger near the hole of the donut and gets weaker as particles get close to the edge. Faster, more energetic particles tend to drift outward and escape, and those fast particles are the best candidates for fusion.

Horizontally oriented magnets help counteract this drift. They wrap around in the other direction. One stack gets placed in the center of the donut and others wrap around the outside. These create a magnetic field that circles around and around the inside of the donut, forcing any particles that drift toward the outside to head back toward the center. As a result, plasma particles are forced to travel around the donut in a spiraling shape.

The most efficient magnetic confinement device, the tokamak, typically uses a donut shape that is taller than it is wide. A cross section of the tube looks like a letter *D*, not like an *O*. Engineers picked this shape for the first large tokamak, JET at the Culham Centre for Fusion Energy, because the flat inner wall made it easier to attach the heavy vertical coils that wrap around the donut. If these coils had been O shaped, their heavy weight would have put too much of a strain on the structure. However, the D shape turned out to do a better job of confining the plasma as well. ITER's reactor will use a D-shaped tube.

It Is Getting Hot in Here ■

Before putting any fusion fuel into a tokamak, engineers must first charge up the magnets and create a vacuum inside the donut-shaped vessel. Once everything is ready, the fuel is injected. In a fusion power plant, this fuel would contain deuterium and tritium gas. In most experimental reactors, it is just deuterium gas. The amount of deuterium the JET tokamak uses for a typical experiment weighs only as much as a postage stamp. But as the gas heats up and becomes a plasma, it expands to fill the entire interior of the donut.

In a tokamak the stack of magnets inside the donut hole also doubles as the source of the electrical energy that generates a current in the plasma. This strong electrical current helps keep the plasma contained and also provides heat. Most people have noticed that wires or power cords tend to become warm or even hot as current flows through them. This is called ohmic heating, and it happens due to electrical resistance. Not all the electricity manages to flow through the conductor. Some particles get stuck, heating up the wire. The

> **WORDS IN CONTEXT**
>
> **ohmic heating**
>
> heating that occurs when an electric current passes through a material

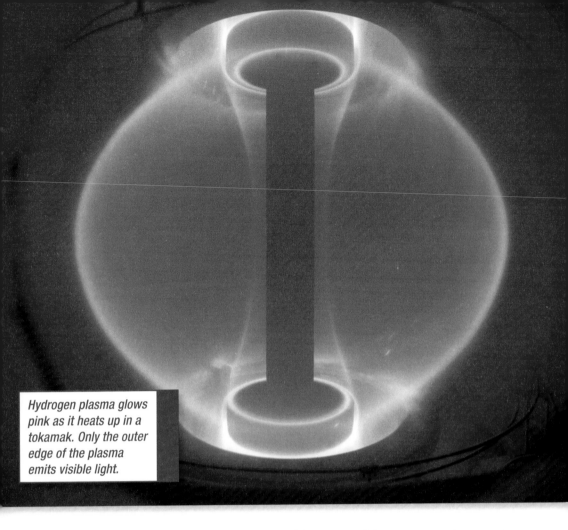

Hydrogen plasma glows pink as it heats up in a tokamak. Only the outer edge of the plasma emits visible light.

same thing happens to plasma. However, this process does not get the plasma hot enough for fusion to occur.

A tokamak also uses neutral beam heating, which is a system that accelerates particles of deuterium to high speeds, then injects them into the plasma. The energy in these beams can be so great that it would vaporize a car in seconds. This extra energy adds heat to the system. A third approach, called radio frequency heating, uses antennae placed along the edge of the plasma to deliver waves of energy at very specific frequencies. These frequencies will be absorbed only by specific particles inside the plasma, providing additional energy to those particles.

As the plasma heats up, it glows pinkish red, a color characteristic of hot hydrogen gas. However, only the relatively cool edge of the plasma glows. The extremely hot central region of the flowing plasma emits no visible light. It is here that fusion reactions will begin to take place, as long as deuterium-tritium fuel is used and the temperature exceeds 180 million degrees F (100 million degrees C). Ignition is reached when these fusion reactions add enough extra heat to the system to make external heating systems unnecessary. Experimental tokamaks have not yet reached ignition.

Super Cool Magnets ■

Current tokamaks operate in pulses that last from around thirty seconds to a few minutes at a time. A magnetic confinement power plant would have to be able to operate either continuously or in pulses that are several hours long. The pulse length is limited by the innermost stack of magnetic coils. These must continually increase their own current in order to generate and maintain a current in the plasma. After thirty seconds or so, these coils reach their maximum current, meaning that the plasma will begin to lose energy and the pulse will cease.

In addition, as these coils carry higher and higher currents, they get hotter and hotter due to electrical resistance. This is the same effect that helps provide heat in the plasma. But it is not helpful at all in the magnets. Cooling systems must circulate water or another coolant around the magnets to keep them from getting too hot. And these cooling processes use up a lot of energy.

To efficiently produce energy, ITER and future fusion power plants will rely on a cutting edge technology: superconducting magnets. A superconducting magnet is made of tight coils of superconducting wire. This wire is formed from mixtures of metals such as niobium and titanium or niobium and tin. When cooled below a certain temperature, a superconducting wire carries electricity with zero electrical resistance.

> WORDS IN CONTEXT
>
> **superconducting**
>
> able to transmit electricity with zero resistance, but only at extremely cold temperatures

The lack of electrical resistance means that superconducting magnets can create more powerful magnetic fields while using up less electricity, because none of the current will be lost to resistance. In addition, the current flowing through superconducting magnets does not heat them up. The magnets still require cooling, though, because superconductivity only works at temperatures close to absolute zero. But in a large fusion reactor such as ITER, the total energy needed to power up and cool superconducting magnets turns out to be much less than that required to run normal magnets.

Each of ITER's eighteen D-shaped superconducting magnets will be 46 feet (14 m) tall and weigh as much as a jumbo jet. A cryogenic plant at ITER will circulate liquid helium through these massive magnets in order to keep them at a constant temperature of -454°F (-270°C). That is also the average temperature of deep space and is over three times colder than the coldest temperature ever recorded in Antarctica. Amazingly, in a fusion reactor, this insanely cold temperature must be maintained just a few feet away from plasma that burns hotter than the sun.

A Twisted Donut ■

Engineers have tried a variety of designs for magnetic confinement devices all based on the donut concept. While the tokamak has led the pack for decades, other variations show promise as well. The strangest of all is the stellarator. In a stellarator the tube itself is twisted into a spiral and covered with magnets that twist and bend as well. The result is a structure that looks like it used to be shaped like a donut but went through the dryer and got terribly wrinkled.

The twisted magnets form the perfect cage for the plasma. As a result, a stellarator does not need to apply a current to the plasma. Producing that current is what limits a tokamak to brief pulses of operation. Without that limitation, a stellarator should be able to keep hot plasma flowing and confined for up to thirty minutes at a time. In addition, stellarators are not prone to disruptions, a plasma instability that plagues tokamaks. The downside is that planning and building the twisted structure of a stellarator is an engineering nightmare.

The Princeton Plasma Physics Laboratory in New Jersey started building a stellarator in 2004, but the project was canceled

Kicking It into H-Mode

One of the greatest discoveries in the history of magnetic fusion research happened accidentally. In 1982 German physicist Fritz Wagner noticed during a series of experiments that he could get the ornery plasma to behave much better. He just had to start with a high enough plasma density and then add intense neutral beam heating. The result was a plasma that stayed hot and dense for a longer duration than ever before. "It came out of nothing. It wasn't predicted, it just happened," Wagner recalled many years later. Physicists called the discovery high-confinement mode, or H-mode for short. In H-mode the plasma generates an edge that curtails turbulence and helps prevent particles from escaping. It was an island of unexpected stability in the midst of a stormy plasma sea. If H-mode did not exist, ITER's reactor would have to be twice as large in order to produce the same amount of energy.

Quoted in Robert Arnoux, "How Fritz Wagner 'Discovered' the H-Mode," *ITER Newsline*, June 19, 2009. www.iter.org.

in 2008 after the cost rose much higher than expected due to the difficulty of the construction. Another stellarator project came close to cancellation but pulled through. In December 2015 the largest stellarator ever built, Wendelstein 7-X, switched on for the first time at the Max Planck Institute for Plasma Physics in Greifswald, Germany. Engineers had used a supercomputer to design the complex twisting shapes of the plasma tube and the fifty magnetic coils that surround it. Computers also controlled the welding of the components to ensure each piece was shaped to within a millimeter of the required dimensions. It took nine years and 1.1 million construction hours, but the machine was finally finished.

Engineers loaded Wendelstein 7-X with helium plasma for its first series of runs, since this plasma is easier to create and control than one made from hydrogen. Everything went smoothly. "This was really the beginning, and the machine works nicely. The confinement time was very large, we knew we were on the right path,"[31] says Hans-Stephan Bosch of the Max Planck Institute. After running the device with hydrogen plasma as well, engineers

Germany's Wendelstein 7-X (shown) is the world's largest stellarator, a type of fusion reactor. A supercomputer was used to design its complex array of twisted tubing surrounded by magnetic coils.

shut the stellarator down for modifications to prepare it for operation with deuterium. This next phase, which should begin in 2019, will produce fusion reactions, but the team does not expect to pass breakeven. The experiments are more of a proof of concept than an attempt to produce energy.

Shrinking in Scale ■

The rule for tokamak success has always been that bigger is better. That is why ITER's reactor will be so massive. However, bigger devices take a lot more time and money to build. So, many scientists and engineers around the world are experimenting with variations on the traditional tokamak design, hoping to find a way to achieve success on a smaller scale.

At Skunk Works, a research team sponsored by the defense giant Lockheed Martin and based in California, scientists are working on what they call a compact fusion reactor. It has the potential to produce the same energy as a tokamak ten times its size. The small size is key to their approach, says Thomas McGuire, lead engineer for the project. "It's one of the reasons we think it is feasible for development and future economics,"[32] he notes. McGuire first started looking into small fusion reactors in graduate school as a potential way to propel spacecraft. Instead of forcing plasma to travel in a ring around a donut-shaped reactor, this small machine uses superconducting coils to create a powerful magnetic border around a chamber. The plasma spreads out in the middle, filling the whole chamber.

Another promising alternative to the tokamak fattens up the donut shape. The spherical tokamak resembles a cored apple. This altered shape allows the device to use less-powerful magnetic fields to obtain the same plasma pressure as a regular tokamak. In other words, the device offers more bang for the buck when it comes to magnet strength. As a result, spherical tokamaks can be smaller in size. "The aim is to make tokamaks smaller, cheaper, and faster—to reduce the eventual cost of electricity,"[33] says Ian Chapman of the Culham Centre for Fusion Energy.

The new approach has its downsides, however. Howard Wilson of the York Plasma Institute at the University of York in the United Kingdom says, "Spherical tokamaks are the new kids on the block. But there are still important questions we're trying to get to the bottom of."[34] For example, it is very difficult to fit superconducting magnets into the slim central column of a spherical tokamak. As a result, these devices are limited to less-powerful magnets.

Still, several experimental spherical tokamaks are currently in operation, including the Mega Amp Spherical Tokamak at the Culham Centre for Fusion Energy and the National Spherical Torus Experiment at the Princeton Plasma Physics Laboratory.

A private company based in the United Kingdom, Tokamak Energy, is building a new spherical tokamak named ST-40. The company hopes to prove that energy from fusion is possible with small, compact machines. "Fusion projects in government laboratories have become increasingly expensive and slow," says chief executive officer David Kingham, referring to ITER's numerous delays. "However, now there is a new way forward with fusion, based on rapid development of new technologies by private ventures. . . . We feel that we can make fusion a reality [and start] putting fusion electricity into the grid by 2030,"[35] he said.

Even Mightier Magnets ■

Kingham's company is also planning to incorporate cutting-edge high-temperature superconducting magnets into its new device. These kinds of magnets did not yet exist when ITER's planning and construction began. These magnets will use superconducting materials that function at slightly higher temperatures than traditional superconductors. This will make them easier and cheaper to work with than regular superconductors. Most important, the new high-temperature superconductors can handle the very strong magnetic fields needed to produce fusion energy. This new technology has the potential to nearly double the strength of the magnetic fields in a tokamak. With magnets such as these, a fusion reactor the size of JET could theoretically put out 500 MW of fusion power—the same amount ITER hopes to produce.

In 2015 students at MIT designed a small fusion reactor they called ARC, standing for affordable, robust, and compact. It was based on these high-temperature, high-magnetic-field superconductors. Their device should be able to produce three times as much energy as it consumes, but as of 2017 it remains a conceptual exercise. "Going to higher magnetic fields . . . can lead to much smaller (and hence cheaper and quicker-to-build) devices,"[36] says Kingham. These new magnets can also keep plasma confined for a much longer pulse than ever before. In 2015 Tokamak Energy's ST25 HTS device maintained a plasma continuously for twenty-nine hours.

The MIT team and Tokamak Energy are not alone. Numerous research groups and small companies around the globe think they can beat the Goliath that is ITER to the fusion prize, using technical cunning to outpace the giant. It is anyone's guess who will be the first to make fusion energy a reality. Perhaps more than one method will win out. The laser fusion scientists have not given up yet. "I'm convinced that both approaches, magnetic and inertial, will be realized," says Mike Dunne of the Central Laser Facility. "Considering the energy challenge, we need as many solutions as we can deliver."[37]

CHAPTER 5

SOLUTIONS: Cold Fusion and Fringe Science

"The big labs have shown that fusion is doable, and now there are small companies that are thinking about that, and they say, it's not that it cannot be done, but it's how to make it cost-effectively."

—Michel Laberge, founder of General Fusion

Michel Laberge, "How Synchronized Hammer Strikes Could Generate Nuclear Fusion," transcript, TED, April 2014. www.ted.com.

Something strange happened at chemist Stanley Pons's lab at the University of Utah in 1989. He had left a small glass device called an electrolytic cell running overnight. The device used electrodes to pass an electric current through heavy water, which contains deuterium. The next day Pons found that his device had blown up, and he deduced that the energy that destroyed the cell must have come from fusion reactions. He and his collaborator, Martin Fleischmann of the University of Southampton in England, soon announced their discovery, which came to be known as "cold fusion." They claimed the cell could produce up to 100 percent more energy than it took in.

Cold fusion reactions seemed to be happening at room temperature, in a device simple and cheap enough to be built in a high school science laboratory. Supposedly, fusion was happening inside the electrodes, which were made of palladium, a metal. When the electric charge flowed, it split the water molecules apart, and deuterium atoms got absorbed into the metal. Over a time period of ten hours or more, Pons said, some of these atoms would fuse thanks to an effect of quantum mechanics known as quantum tunneling.

At the American Chemical Society meeting that year, thousands of chemists applauded the discovery. Some news media reported that the world's energy problems were over. "Break-through process has potential to provide inexhaustible source of energy,"[38] said one headline. However, physicists remained skeptical. The news seemed too good to be true. Decades of fusion research had shown that fusion should only happen at temperatures over 180 million degrees F (100 million degrees C). A fusion expert who did not wish to be identified by name told the *New York Times*, "I don't know what he and Fleischmann are seeing, but until someone else does the experiment for all to see, I think we must be very wary of the claim."[39]

Within a few months, Nathan Lewis, a physicist at the California Institute of Technology, had thoroughly tested the claim by repeating the original experiment multiple times. He was unable to reproduce the results, and he concluded that the original experimental setup had most likely included mistakes. Regarding the explosion, Lewis said, "I understand that someone turned the current off for a while. When that happens hydrogen naturally bubbles out of the palladium cathode, and creates a hazard of fire or explosion. It is a simple chemical reaction that has nothing to do with fusion."[40]

Stanley Pons (right) and Martin Fleischmann (left), shown here in 1993, are credited with discovering cold fusion. The two scientists claim that the process could produce up to twice as much energy as it takes in.

"A Miracle Machine" ■

In the end cold fusion became synonymous with bad science, and in 1999 *Time* magazine included it as one of the one hundred worst ideas of the twentieth century. The reputations of Pons and Fleischmann were ruined. But dreams of easy access to fusion energy have not gone away. Some scientists continue to study electrolytic cells like the one that set off the whole controversy. Some are still convinced that nuclear reactions are occurring. Because of the bad press associated with the name *cold fusion*, the phenomenon has been rebranded as low-energy nuclear reactions, or LENR.

Some universities, businesses, and reputable organizations, including the National Aeronautics and Space Administration (NASA), have gotten involved in research in this field, but the results are still unclear. "While I personally find sufficient demonstration that LENR effects warrant further investigation, I remain skeptical," says Joe Zawodny of NASA, who has worked in this area. "Furthermore, I am unaware of any clear and convincing

The Fusion Conspiracy

An underground community of believers thinks that cold fusion is real but that the truth about this miraculous discovery is being suppressed. One version of the story is that the coal, oil, gas, and nuclear industries do not want the public to have access to cheap energy, so they purposefully discredited Pons and Fleischmann's discovery. Others say that cold fusion broke the laws of physics, so the scientific community refused to accept it as fact. Or scientists did not want to lose funding for hot fusion research, so they mocked cold fusion to limit its funding.

Cold fusion conspiracy theories are closely related to theories about other seemingly miraculous inventions that have supposedly been kept from the public. The general term for any of these theories is a "free energy suppression conspiracy." All of these various theories hinge on the belief that powerful people somehow have the ability to keep a major discovery from getting out as public knowledge.

demonstrations of any viable commercial device producing useful amounts of net energy."[41]

Italian inventor Andrea Rossi says that he has developed such a device. He claims that his Energy Catalyzer, or E-Cat for short, can produce excess heat through low-energy nuclear reactions. The details of how the device works are shrouded in secrecy, but the basics include adding hydrogen gas to powdered nickel, then heating up the concoction. This supposedly fuses some of the nickel and hydrogen into copper, producing more heat energy than was put into the system. However, many physicists believe these results to be impossible.

Rossi and his invention became the subject of a lawsuit that brought into focus the many questions surrounding the viability of the E-Cat. Though Rossi has some followers who believe he has been treated unfairly, mainstream scientists are skeptical. As the famous astronomer Carl Sagan liked to say, "Extraordinary claims require extraordinary evidence,"[42] and there just is not enough evidence that the E-Cat or any other cold fusion device is a miracle machine.

Bursting Bubbles ■

Yet another fusion-related scandal shook the scientific community in 2002. Again, researchers claimed to have observed fusion happening in a small, relatively simple experimental setup. Rusi P. Taleyarkhan, who worked for Oak Ridge National Laboratory at the time, and Richard T. Lahey Jr. of Rensselaer Polytechnic Institute in New York said that they had produced fusion using sound waves to pop bubbles inside a liquid solution. "It is not an easy experiment to run, despite its apparent simplicity," write Taleyarkhan and Lahey. "It took us two and a half years of painstaking experimentation—and dozens of broken flasks—to observe fusion."[43] Their paper was reviewed by fellow scientists and published in a reputable journal, but other scientists were quick to dismiss the results. Some said it was like the cold fusion fiasco happening all over again.

However, there was one important difference. The bubble-popping process could, for a brief instant, produce temperatures and pressures high enough to cause fusion. From a scientific perspective, bubble fusion was not impossible, just unlikely. Bubble fusion, also known as sonofusion, is based on a known physical phenomenon called sonoluminescence. This happens when sound waves jiggle tiny bubbles of gas inside a liquid. As a result, the bubbles grow, then collapse suddenly. Each collapse is energetic enough to produce a quick flash of visible light and perhaps to fuse atoms. The collapsing bubble is somewhat similar to the implosion that drives the nuclear reactions in laser fusion. A Purdue University scientific committee ultimately concluded that Taleyarkhan had engaged in research misconduct. Nevertheless, other groups of researchers are investigating the process. Some have taken bubble fusion to the next level.

The company First Light Fusion, based in the United Kingdom, uses high-tech equipment to generate intense shock waves in order to crush gas-filled bubbles. The company claims to have formed plasma inside these imploding bubbles. Several other companies, including Burst Energies in Nevada and Nano-Spire Inc. in Maine, are also working on advanced techniques to grow and burst bubbles. They call the technology cavitation. Since these are all private companies, details on how their processes work are scarce.

Mixing Magnets and Lasers ■
Cold fusion and bubble fusion are both clouded with controversy. However, plenty of other scientifically feasible approaches to fusion energy exist. The company General Fusion in Canada is working on a technique called magnetized target fusion. "It's a bit of a mix between a magnetized fusion and the laser fusion,"[44] says General Fusion founder Michel Laberge. The Los Alamos National Laboratory in New Mexico has also worked on this approach in the past.

The process starts by spinning liquid metal around to create a vortex down the middle, like the vortex in water as it swirls down the drain. Then a ball of warm, charged plasma is dropped into the opening. The current flowing through the plasma keeps it confined, just as in magnetic confinement fusion. Next a whole bunch of pistons—as many as three hundred—slam into the device, like hammers whacking its sides. This sends shock waves through the liquid metal to compress and heat the plasma, just as in laser fusion. With enough heat and compression, fusion will occur in the plasma. The device is still a work in progress, says Laberge. "We're testing seals, pumping, creating shock waves— getting to know the technology."[45]

Magneto-inertial fusion is yet another mash-up of the two more common techniques. The Z machine at Sandia National Laboratories in Albuquerque, New Mexico, uses powerful electrical currents and their associated magnetic fields to produce incredibly high temperatures and pressures. First, the machine takes about two minutes to charge up. It gathers the amount of electrical energy that a 100-watt lightbulb would use if it stayed on for two days. But when the Z machine fires, it releases all that energy in less than one hundred nanoseconds. This is called a Z pinch. Because the release is so quick, it can generate 80 trillion watts at once, which is around the same power as a strong bolt of lightning.

A strong bolt of lightning produces about 80 trillion watts of energy, which is about the same as the so-called Z pinch produces in the magneto-inertial fusion process. The Z pinch releases all that energy in less than one hundred nanoseconds.

Just as in laser fusion, all this energy focuses on a cylindrical capsule containing fusion fuel. Unlike laser fusion, the Z pinch sends a powerful electrical current through the cylinder. This forms a magnetic field wrapping around the capsule, forcing it to implode and compress the fuel inside. At the moment compression begins, a laser shines into the fuel to heat it up. During the implosion, the fuel experiences enough heat and density to fuse. Sandia Laboratories began introducing tritium to the fuel mixture in 2016. Their computer simulations show that they should be able to achieve breakeven on the machine.

Alternative Fuels ■

A private company, Helion Energy in Washington State, is also investigating a form of magneto-inertial fusion sometimes called colliding-beam fusion. This group's approach involves firing two rings of plasma at each other using pulsed magnetic fields. The plasma rings merge, then a strong magnetic field compresses the plasma to the required temperature and pressure. Helion Energy plans to keep its device to a manageable size, about as big as a semitruck. The company plans to fuse deuterium with helium-3 instead of tritium.

Another company, Tri Alpha Energy in California, is also working on colliding-beam fusion using a different type of fuel—a mix of hydrogen and boron. Fusing these alternative fuels requires much higher temperatures than it takes to fuse deuterium and tritium. But alternative fuels may be more practical in the long run. The main drawback of using deuterium and tritium is that these fuels produce high-energy neutrons when they react. These particles slam into the walls of the reactor, making it radioactive and introducing impurities into the plasma. To avoid these and other complications, Tri Alpha Energy has set its sights on producing the 5.4 billion degrees F (3 billion degrees C) temperature required to fuse hydrogen and boron.

Tri Alpha Energy's machine is the length of two buses parked end to end. Just like Helion Energy's device, it begins by firing two rings of plasma at each other. But it does not then compress the plasma. Rather, it attempts to confine it with magnetic fields long enough for fusion to occur. So far, the plasma has lasted for about five milliseconds. That is not very long—an eye blink lasts about one hundred milliseconds. The company must produce higher temperatures and longer confinement times before the technique can succeed. In order to do so, Tri Alpha Energy has begun taking apart its current machine to build a bigger and better version.

A third company, Lawrenceville Plasma Physics in New Jersey, also plans to fuse hydrogen and boron. Founder Eric Lerner calls his approach focus fusion. This approach exploits known plasma instabilities, harnessing them to create a tiny ball of dense, high-temperature plasma where fusion can occur. Lerner says that his device has achieved high enough temperatures for fusion, but density remains an issue.

From Experiment to Power Plant ■

All of these ideas sound great on paper. But it remains to be seen which, if any, has what it takes to provide energy from fusion on a commercial scale. Most laser fusion and tokamak projects,

Fusors for Energy

The fusor is perhaps the simplest of all fusion devices—it was the variety teen genius Taylor Wilson built. A fusor uses electric fields to heat and confine plasma. While handy for producing neutrons, this device consumes more energy than it provides. It uses two orbs of wire mesh, one inside the other, to transfer a voltage that drives the plasma toward the center of the device. However, particles tend to get caught on the wire mesh and absorbed before they can fuse. Physicist Robert Bussard thought he could improve the design and turn the device into a power generator. The result was the Polywell, which he first introduced in the 1980s. It replaces the wire mesh arrangement with invisible magnetic fields that set up a trap for positively charged particles in the very center of the device. Though Bussard has since passed away, his idea lives on as the company EMC2 Fusion Development Corporation.

including ITER, have been developed with the goal of reaching ignition. They do not have the capability of supplying electricity to the grid. And transforming an experimental fusion reactor into a machine that produces electricity is not easy. What works in a carefully controlled laboratory setting may not work in a power plant. A power plant must be able to reliably supply electricity to the grid without frequent shutdowns for repairs or maintenance. A power plant must also be able to withstand years of operation. In an inertial confinement fusion reactor, each burst of power is like a tiny bomb exploding. In a magnetic confinement device, the plasma burns hotter than the sun and spits out particles

This fission-process nuclear power plant reliably produces a steady output of electricity. As scientists close in on creating a well-functioning fusion reactor, they will still have to figure out how to apply it for everyday use in a power plant.

that make any nearby materials radioactive. These conditions put extreme stress on the structure of the reactor. Researchers must carefully test all materials to be used in the construction of a fusion power plant.

Alternative fuels, such as the ones proposed by Helion Energy, Tri Alpha Energy, and Lawrenceville Plasma Physics, may be necessary to avoid the radioactivity and impurities introduced by the deuterium-tritium reaction. Also, tritium itself is radioactive and does not occur naturally on Earth. It would have to be produced, most likely at the reactor site, through a process called tritium breeding. This process involves adding a layer of material, called a blanket, along the wall of the reactor. The blanket would contain lithium. When neutrons escaping from fusion reactions hit lithium, it fissions into smaller pieces, including helium and tritium. ITER will not be set up to breed its own tritium, but it will be used to test the process.

A fusion power plant would also need a way to effectively harvest energy from the plasma core. In a tokamak-type plant, the lithium blanket would most likely serve double duty, as it would absorb energy from speedy neutrons exiting the plasma. This would heat up the blanket. That heat would then transfer into a coolant circulating around the reactor. The coolant could be water or some other liquid. Then steam from this hot liquid would turn turbines to produce electricity. Variations of this process are already used in nuclear fission power plants today.

Once a fusion reactor reaches ignition in experimental conditions, the next step will be to build a prototype of a fusion power plant that produces electricity. This will demonstrate whether companies will be able to afford to build and operate such a plant. In order to provide energy to the world, fusion must be able to compete with other forms of power.

Though fusion power has remained just out of reach for decades, governments, companies, and private investors continue to pour money into fusion research. Scientists and engineers keep making improvements to their techniques and developing and testing new ideas. They carry on this work because the promise of fusion energy is so tantalizing. Clayton Myers, a physicist at the Princeton Plasma Physics Laboratory, says, "It almost sounds too good to be true: this concept that we're going to have a limitless, carbon-free energy source. But the nuclear physics says that it's not. It is proven that fusion reactions are real and that we can make them."[46]

Fusion energy would not contribute to climate change. It would not pollute the environment. It would draw its fuel from seawater. And it has the potential to create more energy from simple seawater than any other form of energy production used today. Fusion science promises that one day, humans will have their very own stars here on Earth.

SOURCE NOTES

INTRODUCTION
"A Sun in a Bottle"

1. Quoted in Dino Grandoni, "Why It's Taking the U.S. So Long to Make Fusion Energy Work," *Huffington Post*, January 20, 2015. www.huffingtonpost.com.
2. Quoted in Tom Clynes, *The Boy Who Played with Fusion*. New York: Houghton Mifflin Harcourt, 2015, p. 103.

CHAPTER 1
CURRENT STATUS: Nuclear Energy

3. Quoted in Tom Clynes, "The Boy Who Played with Fusion," *Popular Science*, February 14, 2012. www.popsci.com.
4. Quoted in John Stang, "Energy's Holy Grail? You Can Find It at Redmond's Helion Energy," Crosscut.com, January 20, 2015. http://crosscut.com.
5. Quoted in Joseph Mcclain, "Safer, More Efficient, Fusion-Generated Electricity Is on the Horizon," Phys.org, October 12, 2012. www.emc2-explained.info.
6. Quoted in Daniel Clery, *A Piece of the Sun: The Quest for Fusion Energy*. New York and London: Overlook Duckworth, 2013, p. 42.
7. Quoted in Clynes, *The Boy Who Played with Fusion*, pp. 96, 64.
8. Quoted in Clynes, "The Boy Who Played with Fusion," *Popular Science*.
9. Quoted in Clynes, *The Boy Who Played with Fusion*, p. 106.
10. Quoted in Clynes, *The Boy Who Played with Fusion*, p. 106.

CHAPTER 2
PROBLEMS: Breaking Even and Scaling Up

11. Quoted in EuroFusion, "50 Years of Lawson Criteria," 2005. www.euro-fusion.org.
12. Quoted in EuroFusion. "Interview with JD Lawson," 2005. www.euro-fusion.org.

13. Quoted in Culham Centre for Fusion Energy, "Taming the ELMs," 2012. www.ccfe.ac.uk.

14. Quoted in Lynne Degitz, "Disruption Researchers Investigate Design Options," *ITER Newsline*, January 14, 2013. www.iter .org.

15. Quoted in Culham Centre for Fusion Energy. "Taming the ELMs."

16. Quoted in David Biello, "High-Powered Lasers Deliver Fusion Energy Breakthrough," *Scientific American*, February 12, 2014. www.scientificamerican.com.

17. Quoted in Rachel Feltman, "Why Don't We Have Fusion Power?," *Popular Mechanics*, May 16, 2013. www.popularme chanics.com.

18. Quoted in Feltman, "Why Don't We Have Fusion Power?"

CHAPTER 3
SOLUTIONS: Zap It with Lasers

19. Quoted in Adam Mann, "We're One Step Closer to Nuclear Fusion Energy," *Wired*, February 12, 2014. www.wired.com.

20. Quoted in Biello, "High-Powered Lasers Deliver Fusion Energy Breakthrough."

21. Quoted in Akshat Rathi, "Big Leap for Fusion: More Energy Produced than Spent Igniting Fuel," Ars Technica, February 12, 2014. https://arstechnica.com.

22. Quoted in Lawrence Livermore National Laboratory, "NIF Construction." https://lasers.llnl.gov.

23. Quoted in University of Rochester, "A First for Direct-Drive Fusion," September 6, 2016. www.rochester.edu.

24. Quoted in Melinda Rose, "Laser Fusion: The Uncertain Road to Ignition," *Optics & Photonics News*, September 2014. www.osa-opn.org.

25. Quoted in Rose, "Laser Fusion."

26. Quoted in Rose, "Laser Fusion."

27. Quoted in Rose, "Laser Fusion."

28. Quoted in Kenneth Chang, "Machinery of an Energy Dream," *New York Times*, March 17, 2014. www.nytimes.com.

CHAPTER 4
SOLUTIONS: Wrap It with Magnets

29. Quoted in Davide Castelvecchi and Jeff Tollefson, "US Advised to Stick with Troubled Fusion Reactor ITER," *Nature*, May 26, 2016. www.nature.com.

30. Quoted in David Chandler, "MIT Tests Unique Approach to Fusion Power," *MIT News*, March 19, 2008. http://news.mit.edu.

31. Quoted in Alexander Hellemans, "Fusion Stellarator Wendelstein 7-X Fires Up for Real." *IEEE Spectrum*, February 3, 2016. http://spectrum.ieee.org.

32. Quoted in Guy Norris, "Skunk Works Reveals Compact Fusion Reactor Details," *Aviation Week*, October 15, 2014. http://aviationweek.com.

33. Quoted in Dan Clery, "The New Shape of Fusion," *Science*, May 22, 2015. http://science.sciencemag.org.

34. Quoted in Clery, "The New Shape of Fusion."

35. Quoted in World Nuclear News, "Spherical Tokamak 'to Put Fusion Power in Grid' by 2030," January 30, 2017. www.world-nuclear-news.org.

36. Quoted in David L. Chandler, "A Small, Modular, Efficient Fusion Plant," *MIT News*, August 10, 2015. http://news.mit.edu.

37. Quoted in Robert Arnoux, "HiPER—the Other Way to Fusion Energy," *ITER Newsline*, October 2, 2009. www.iter.org.

CHAPTER 5
SOLUTIONS: Cold Fusion and Fringe Science

38. Quoted in Charles Platt, "What If Cold Fusion Is Real?," *Wired*, November 1, 1998. www.wired.com.

39. Quoted in Malcolm W. Browne, "Fusion in a Jar: Announcement by 2 Chemists Ignites Uproar," *New York Times*, March 28, 1989. www.nytimes.com.

40. Quoted in Malcolm W. Browne, "Physicists Debunk Claim of a New Kind of Fusion," *New York Times*, May 3, 1989. http://partners.nytimes.com.

41. Joe Zawodny, "Technology Gateway Video," *Joe Zawodny: Observations* (blog), January 14, 2012. http://joe.zawodny.com.

42. Quoted in David Deming, "Do Extraordinary Claims Require Extraordinary Evidence?," *Philosophia*, October 20, 2016. https://link.springer.com.

43. Richard T. Lahey Jr., Rusi P. Taleyarkhan, and Robert I. Nigamatulin, "Bubble Power," *IEEE Spectrum*, May 2, 2005. http://spectrum.ieee.org.

44. Michel Laberge, "How Synchronized Hammer Strikes Could Generate Nuclear Fusion," transcript, TED, April 2014. www.ted.com.

45. Quoted in Dan Clery, "Fusion's Restless Pioneers," *Science*, July 25, 2014. http://science.sciencemag.org.

46. Quoted in Maddie Stone, "The Real Problem with Fusion Energy," Gizmodo, May 27, 2016. http://gizmodo.com.

FIND OUT MORE

Books

Daniel Clery, *A Piece of the Sun: The Quest for Fusion Energy*. New York and London: Overlook Duckworth, 2013.

Tom Clynes, *The Boy Who Played with Fusion*. New York: Houghton Mifflin Harcourt, 2015.

Gary McCracken and Peter Stott, *Fusion: The Energy of the Universe*. Burlington, MA: Elsevier Academic, 2012.

Charles Seife, *Sun in a Bottle: The Strange History of Fusion and the Science of Wishful Thinking*. New York: Viking, 2008.

US Government Department of Energy, *Nuclear Fusion Energy Encyclopedia*. (Kindle edition), Progressive Management, 2014.

Websites

Culham Centre for Fusion Energy (www.ccfe.ac.uk). The center is home to JET and the Mega Amp Spherical Tokamak, two of the world's most important tokamaks. Its website contains a wealth of information on both of these devices as well as fusion energy in general. The organization also hosts a YouTube channel, CulhamFusionEnergy, with educational videos on fusion.

EuroFusion (www.euro-fusion.org). This organization manages and funds fusion research throughout Europe. The site includes excellent resources on how fusion energy works, both on Earth and in the sun. Look in the Multimedia section for a game called Operation Tokamak, in which players attempt to keep a tokamak running.

Fusor.net (http://fusor.net). This online community brings together people interested in building their own fusion reactors. The site provides technical resources as well as encouragement and support to fusioneers. It also maintains a hall of fame mentioning the names of all those who have achieved fusion.

ITER (www.iter.org). Learn more about the world's most expensive scientific machine, currently under construction in France. The International Thermonuclear Experimental Reactor will be the largest tokamak ever built, and it is expected to reach ignition.

Internet Sources

David Biello, "High-Powered Lasers Deliver Fusion Energy Breakthrough," *Scientific American*, February 12, 2014. www.scientific american.com/article/high-powered-lasers-deliver-fusion-energy -breakthrough.

Kenneth Chang, "Machinery of an Energy Dream," *New York Times*, March 17, 2013. www.nytimes.com/2014/03/18/science /the-challenge-how-to-keep-fusion-going-long-enough.html?_r=1.

Dan Clery, "Fusion's Restless Pioneers," *Science*, July 25, 2014. http://science.sciencemag.org/content/345/6195/370.full.

Dan Clery, "The New Shape of Fusion," *Science*, May 22, 2015. http://science.sciencemag.org/content/348/6237/854.full.

Raffi Khatchadourian, "A Star in a Bottle." *New Yorker*, March 3, 2014. www.newyorker.com/magazine/2014/03/03/a-star-in-a-bottle.

Melinda Rose, "Laser Fusion: The Uncertain Road to Ignition," *Optics & Photonics News*, September 2014. www.osapublishing .org/opn/abstract.cfm?uri=opn-25-9-34.

INDEX

ABOUT THE AUTHOR

Kathryn Hulick is a freelance writer and former Peace Corps volunteer. After returning from two years of teaching English in Kyrgyzstan, she started writing for children. Her books include *Pop Culture: American Life and Video Games*, *Awesome Science: Dinosaurs*, and *Careers in Robotics*. She also contributes regularly to *Muse* magazine and the Science News for Students website. She enjoys hiking, painting, reading, and working in her garden, where fusion in the sun provides energy for vegetables and flowers. She lives in Massachusetts with her husband and son.